I0108818

MASTERING SIN

Winning the Battle Against the
Fallen Adamic Nature

Malachi C. Steele

MASTERING SIN. Copyright © 2023. Malachi C. Steele.

All rights reserved. No portion of this book may be reproduced, stored in a retrieval system, or transmitted in any form or by any means – electronic, mechanical, photocopy, recording, scanning or other – except for a brief quotation in critical reviews or articles, without the prior written permission of the publisher or author.

Published by:

Connect with the author @ malachicsteele@gmail.com

ISBN: 978-1-958404-39-3 (paperback)

Scripture quotations marked "NKJV" are taken from the New King James Version. Copyright © 1982 by Thomas Nelson, Inc. Used by permission. All rights reserved. Bible text from the New King James Version® is not to be reproduced in copies or otherwise by any means except as permitted in writing by Thomas Nelson, Inc., Attn: Bible Rights and Permissions, P.O. Box 141000, Nashville, TN 37214-1000.

Scripture quotations marked (NLT) are taken from the Holy Bible, New Living Translation, copyright © 1996, 2004, 2007 by Tyndale House Foundation. Used by permission of

Tyndale House Publishers, Inc., Carol Stream, Illinois 60188. All rights reserved.

Scripture quotations taken from the Amplified® Bible (AMP). Copyright © 2015 by The Lockman Foundation. Used by permission. www.Lockman.org.

You will be accepted if you do what is right. But if you refuse to do what is right, then watch out! Sin is crouching at the door, eager to control you. But you must subdue it and be its master. (Genesis 4:7 - NLT).

Preface

I have read many stories of people who have overcome their "animal instincts" or "animal soul" or "lower self," whatever we want to call it. I know it as the "adamic nature" or the "sinful nature." These produce desires that emanate from within for that which we know is blatant sin.

As a married man, I have been tempted by other women and have wondered how a strong and potent desire can be for something so wrong. Oh, how we want to hear the Father say, "It is not wrong. Go ahead and indulge." But such sentiments are not forthcoming from our God, who is the epitome and full embodiment of holiness.

The journey for the believer is not to survive the world but to overcome it. The path Jesus traveled was always the path for the fallen man, but I believe we have resolved, after repeated failed attempts, that it was impossible until Jesus came and proved that it wasn't. Many have settled their resolve that only Jesus alone could have done it.

When Jesus called Peter off the boat to walk on water, most of the people on the boat could not conceive of the idea that if Jesus was walking on water, maybe they could too. Only one responded to the invitation. Only one thought and reached out and made an attempt. Jesus gladly obliged, and Peter did walk on water, even if it was only a few steps.

What Jesus did on our behalf does not absolve us of our responsibility to create and destroy, and that is what this whole idea of mastering sin is all about. Jesus did not just make it possible; He proved that it was.

Table of Contents

Introduction

This is going to be a very interesting conversation, but before we begin, there is one thing I want you to keep in mind: As you study Scripture, particularly, the New Testament or, rightly put, the New Covenant, the letters of Paul were written to the church. It means then that the works of the flesh, as outlined by him, was a challenge for believers, not unbelievers. In other words, the church, though saved, sanctified, and filled with the Holy Ghost, still had a sin problem.

I grew up in church, got saved in my late teenage years, was filled with the Holy Spirit soon thereafter, and still struggled with sin. I thought something was seriously wrong with me as the Bible says in John that a son of God does not sin (see 1 John 3:9). The church also teaches that holiness is somehow tied to our capacity to stop sinning. What this mindset has done is cause many believers to live fragmented lives. On the one hand, they are the epitome of holiness, while secretly, they are struggling with some aspect of the fallen Adamic nature. We are shocked when such secrets become public, and the

11

judgment from us is often very harsh, but we are not immune to the same failures. Paul says something very interesting:

Therefore let the one who thinks he stands firm [immune to temptation, being overconfident and self-righteous], take care that he does not fall [into sin and condemnation]. No temptation [regardless of its source] has overtaken or enticed you that is not common to human experience [nor is any temptation unusual or beyond human resistance]; but God is faithful [to His word—He is compassionate and trustworthy], and He will not let you be tempted beyond your ability [to resist], but along with the temptation He [has in the past and is now and] will [always] provide the way out as well, so that you will be able to endure it [without yielding, and will overcome temptation with joy]. (1 Corinthians 10:12-13 - AMP).

We know the possibility is there to live above sin, but how many of us can truly attest to this level of maturity? This is not an easy feat for any of us.

But [like a boxer] I strictly discipline my body and make it my slave, so that, after I have preached [the gospel] to others, I myself will not somehow

be disqualified [as unfit for service]. (1 Corinthians 9:27 - AMP).

So the only way to master sin is to make the body a slave, but to whom must this body be a slave to? For most of us, we think our body is the real version of us, and everything else about us is somehow superficial. But there is a you that is within the you as a body that must become master for you to overcome the Adamic nature embedded within, even as a believer.

The human being, made in the image and likeness of God, was created with certain capabilities. For one, by thought, desire, and action, we open up the possibility of bringing things into existence and shaping/creating realities.

When man fell, these capabilities remained intact. Now that man was "doing" what he was not created to do, man started to create realities that became a serious problem for us.

God told the first recorded murderer that it was his responsibility to "master sin." Man has struggled with this idea to this day.

When God became man, Jesus Christ, many believed it was impossible for Him to sin because He is God. Was it really? Or did Jesus demonstrate a greater truth? That it is indeed possible for man to master sin.

We will explore some deeper revelations on this topic. I may not provide all the answers you are looking for, but if we can know how this process works, we may be one step closer to mastering sin. Indulge me for a brief moment as we explore this topic.

Let's talk.

Chapter One

Defining Sin

L ike the babies born into this generation, *baby sin* wants to rule your life. It wants to control your time and actions, but you must rule over it. You must become its master.

To truly master sin, one must control his/her thoughts and train the will through constant practice and intentionality to make the right decisions; thereby, acting rightly when faced with ungodly desires.

Sin was never God's problem. It is a problem we created for ourselves. Though He has made provisions so when we sin, we can be forgiven and we can make it to heaven, it is still on us to master it. Every translation of Genesis 4:7 puts the onus on us:

- Thou shalt rule over him (sin) KJ21
- But you must master it (AMP)
- But you must rule over it (CSB)

- Sin wants to destroy you, but don't let it (CEV)
- Thou shalt have dominion over it (DRA)
- You must control it (ERV)
- You must master it (GW)
- Take dominion over it (ISV)

You get the picture!

What is sin?

But he who doubts is condemned if he eats, because he does not eat from faith; for whatever is not from faith is sin. (Romans 14:23 - NKJV).

We often think the only real sin is sexual, but unbelief is actually the greatest sin. Unbelief sits at the foundation of all sin. In order to sin, we must believe a lie.

Eve doubted God's Word and acted contrary to His command. Unbelief is the most fertile of all sins because it breeds more unbelief.

Cain did not want to accept that he did not do well. Instead, he wanted to blame someone for his disapproval by God. This is something unbelief does.

It influences us to not take responsibility for our actions. When we do that, the sin of unbelief produces offspring. We could say unbelief is the mother of all sins.

Let's look at a specific listing in Scripture:

Do you not know that the unrighteous will not inherit the kingdom of God? Do not be deceived. Neither <u>fornicators</u>, nor <u>idolaters</u>, nor <u>adulterers</u>, nor <u>homosexuals</u>, nor <u>sodomites</u>, nor <u>thieves</u>, nor <u>covetous</u>, nor <u>drunkards</u>, nor <u>revilers</u>, nor <u>extortioners</u> will inherit the kingdom of God. And such were some of you. But you were washed, but you were sanctified, but you were justified in the name of the Lord Jesus and by the Spirit of our God. All things are lawful for me, but all things are not helpful. All things are lawful for me, but I will not be brought under the power of any. Foods for the stomach and the stomach for foods, but God will destroy both it and them. Now the body is not for <u>sexual immorality</u> but for the Lord, and the Lord for the body. And God both raised up the Lord and will also raise us up by His power. Do you not know that your bodies are members of Christ? Shall I then take the members of Christ and make them members of a harlot? Certainly not! Or do you not know that he who is joined to

17

a harlot is one body with her? For "the two," He says, "shall become one flesh." But he who is joined to the Lord is one spirit with Him. Flee sexual immorality. Every sin that a man does is outside the body, but he who commits sexual immorality sins against his own body. Or do you not know that your body is the temple of the Holy Spirit who is in you, whom you have from God, and you are not your own? For you were bought at a price; therefore glorify God in your body and in your spirit, which are God's. (1 Corinthians 6:9-20 – NKJV – emphasis mine).

It does not get more specific than that.

Sin is also classified as the works of the flesh:

Now the works of the flesh are evident, which are: <u>adultery</u>, <u>fornication</u>, <u>uncleanness</u>, <u>lewdness</u>, <u>idolatry</u>, <u>sorcery</u>, <u>hatred</u>, <u>contentions</u>, <u>jealousies</u>, <u>outbursts of wrath</u>, <u>selfish ambitions</u>, <u>dissensions</u>, <u>heresies</u>, <u>envy</u>, <u>murders</u>, <u>drunkenness</u>, <u>revelries</u>, and the like; of which I tell you beforehand, just as I also told you in time past, that those who practice such things will not inherit the kingdom of God. (Galatians 5:19-21 – NKJV – emphasis mine).

Notice Paul says, "Those who practice such things…" In other words, those who feed these desires by perpetually acting on them.

It is not the one who falls to sin that will not inherit the kingdom but those who are mastered by the full-grown version of these.

Remember, the Bible was not written to unbelievers. It means these existed in the church, and still do. It is the quintessential struggle of every redeemed human being.

We must also consider the seven things that God hates, and hate is a very strong word for a Being who epitomizes love:

These six things the Lord hates, yes, seven are an abomination to Him: a proud look, a lying tongue, hands that shed innocent blood, a heart that devises wicked plans, feet that are swift in running to evil, a false witness who speaks lies, and one who sows discord among brethren. Proverbs 6:16-19 - NKJV).

So, how does Paul conclude? Paul says to walk in the spirit…

I say then: Walk in the Spirit, and you shall not fulfill the lust of the flesh. (Galatians 5:16 - NKJV).

This is a mature state with a total disregard for the realm of the flesh. The one who achieves this level of mastery no longer derives any pleasure from this world but experiences the perpetual joy and pleasures from perpetually living in God's presence.

Even unbelievers have the capacity to master some level of control over their tendency to sin, and achieve some measure of transcendence. How much more the believer who is empowered by the Holy Spirit.

Chapter Two

When Desire Conceives

A postle James paints a very vivid picture of how sin works. Again, he was not addressing unbelievers.

But each one is tempted when he is dragged away, enticed and baited [to commit sin] by his own [worldly] desire (lust, passion). Then when the illicit desire has conceived, it gives birth to sin; and when sin has run its course, it gives birth to death. (James 1:14-15 - AMP).

The struggle is real for unbelievers, and there is work to be done. Christianity is not a passive journey where one sits and waits for a rapture or death, whichever comes first. It is the working out of a reality already completed by Christ but not yet fully experienced in time. So Paul says:

So then, my dear ones, just as you have always obeyed [my instructions with enthusiasm], not

only in my presence, but now much more in my absence, continue to work out your salvation [that is, cultivate it, bring it to full effect, actively pursue spiritual maturity] with awe-inspired fear and trembling [using serious caution and critical self-evaluation to avoid anything that might offend God or discredit the name of Christ]. (Philippians 2:12 - AMP).

So, the reality of the finished work of Christ must be contended for in order to experience its complete reality. This is not automatic when one says yes to Jesus. We say yes to a journey that should take us to transfiguration where our body is transformed, but this will not happen without our fullest participation.

The original word for "salvation" in the above text is "sōtērian" which is translated:

- *deliverance, preservation, safety, salvation*

- *deliverance from the molestation of enemies*

- *in an ethical sense, that which concludes to the soul's safety or salvation*

- *of Messianic salvation*

- *salvation as the present possession of all true Christians*

- *future salvation, the sum of benefits and blessings which the Christians, redeemed from all earthly ills, will enjoy after the visible return of Christ from heaven in the consummated and eternal kingdom of God.*

- *Fourfold salvation: saved from the penalty, power, presence and most importantly the pleasure of sin.*

Sin makes only one promise: *That you will have pleasure and fulfilment without God.*

The struggle is real for us as believers, but it is possible to master sin. How does desire conceive? This happens when we act on the desire.

According to James 1:14-15, When we act, sin is born. Let's call this *baby fornication*, for example. Once this baby is born, it incessantly demands to be fed. What does this baby feed on? The very thing that brought it into existence or to life. The more we feed it, the more it grows. When it is fully grown, it leads to our undoing.

So there are two ways to avoid death:

1. Do not act on your desire to sin.
2. Kill the baby when it is born.

The older the baby gets, the harder it will be to kill it.

Am I not forgiven when I sin? Yes, you are, once the condition is met:

So, as God's own chosen people, who are holy [set apart, sanctified for His purpose] and well-beloved [by God Himself], put on a heart of compassion, kindness, humility, gentleness, and patience [which has the power to endure whatever injustice or unpleasantness comes, with good temper]; bearing graciously with one another, and willingly forgiving each other if one has a cause for complaint against another; just as the Lord has forgiven you, so should you forgive. (Colossians 3:12-13 - AMP).

If we do not extend forgiveness, we will be denied forgiveness. As long as we forgive, forgiveness is available to us, but we can still die from a grown sin. Sin always demands its wages, and the wage of sin is death (see Romans 6:23).

Forgiveness is not an indication that we have mastered sin.

Chapter Three

In The Beginning

When Adam sinned, sin entered the world. Adam's sin brought death, so death spread to everyone, for everyone sinned. (Romans 5:12 - NLT).

When Adam disobeyed God, the Bible said sin came into the world. This is the sin of partaking of knowledge we are not yet ready for that causes us to act contrary to God's will or command.

God said, "Do not eat…"

The Lord God placed the man in the Garden of Eden to tend and watch over it. But the Lord God warned him, "You may freely eat the fruit of every tree in the garden—except the tree of the knowledge of good and evil. If you eat its fruit, you are sure to die." (Genesis 2:15-17 - NLT).

God could give us the entire world, but our human tendency is to gravitate to that one thing we are not permitted to have.

Adam and Eve acted on a desire they had. Was their desire evil? No, it was not. As creatures of free will, there will be desires independent of God. It is when we act on these desires that we sin.

We also see a similar scenario with Cain. This is what God said to him after he carried out his desire to murder his brother:

You will be accepted if you do what is right. But if you refuse to do what is right, then watch out! Sin is crouching at the door, eager to control you. But you must subdue it and be its master. (Genesis 4:7 - NLT).

When Cain acted on his desire to kill, sin was birth. *Baby murder* demanded more blood. Cain's life—by extension the Caananites'—were marred with violence.

Did God forgive Adam and Eve? Yes.
Did God forgive Cain? Yes.
Did God kill the babies that were born? No.

Only by the human will can something of our own creation be destroyed.

Some people are not comfortable with thinking we live in a multi-dimensional reality. It sounds too much like science fiction. The old adage is correct: *Truth is stranger than fiction.* The ego, for example, is our own creation. It is the false version of self that believes it can exist independently of God. In the grand scheme of things, there really is nothing but God, so it means the very idea of separation is also a human, fallen concept.

As we engage in acts we were not created to do, we self-duplicate ourselves, creating little offspring that can only be eliminated by an act of our will.

Though forgiven, sin will still demand its wages. But didn't Jesus become sin for us? Didn't He pay the wages sin demands? Yes, He did in its entirety, but it must be worked out to its fullest reality in our lives. Though saved, we still have a responsibility to learn to master sin.

Remember, Jesus died for the whole world. Every human being's sin was paid for, but we know not everyone will be saved because this gift must be accepted and assimilated in the life of a human being for it to be a reality.

If Jesus became sin and paid the wages sin demands, then there really is no sin in the context of the believer. This means the reality that we still sin could not be explained.

John says the one born of God does not sin, but he says more than that:

My dear children, I am writing this to you so that you will not sin. But if anyone does sin, we have an advocate who pleads our case before the Father. He is Jesus Christ, the one who is truly righteous. (1 John 2:1 - NLT).

Anyone who continues to live in him will not sin. But anyone who keeps on sinning does not know him or understand who he is. (1 John 3:6 - NLT).

I would say the one born of God does not have a genuine desire to live in habitual sin, yet that still would not explain those believers who love God but still sin.

"But if anyone sin…" The possibility of sin in the life of the believer is still there. Does forgiveness free us from the demands of our *child*? No, it doesn't.

So now Paul sheds some light on this issue for us:

I don't really understand myself, for I want to do what is right, but I don't do it. Instead, I do what I hate. But if I know that what I am doing is wrong, this shows that I agree that the law is good. So I am not the one doing wrong; it is sin living in me that does it. And I know that nothing good lives in me, that is, in my sinful nature. I want to do what is right, but I can't. I want to do what is good, but I don't. I don't want to do what is wrong, but I do it anyway. But if I do what I don't want to do, I am not really the one doing wrong; it is sin living in me that does it. (Romans 7:15-20 - NLT).

Paul lived an ascended life. He was caught up in the spirit on many occasions, and even saw and heard things he could not articulate. What could he possibly know about sin?

The one who is born from above (born again) and the *being of sin* are two separate entities rolled into one, and this conflict exists in everyone.

31

Paul says, "I die daily." (see 1 Corinthians 15:31). This is not just an awareness of the dangers of persecution faced by the radical apostles daily, but a statement of fact in regards to a version of self that must be suppressed in order for the true self to fully manifest. It is the destruction of all false ideals, beliefs, and perception of oneself that must be accomplished by the believer working out his own salvation with fear and trembling. It is a necessary battle, and the only battle a believer is commissioned to fight because it is incumbent on the will. Anything having to do with human will is outside God's jurisdiction.

Chapter Four

Breaking It Down

We go back to James' discourse. In order for sin not to be conceived and born, we must will ourselves not to act on our desires that are contrary to the heart of God no matter how we feel compelled to do it.

There is no justifying sin. God will not bend His will to accommodate sin. Trust me, I have tried to get Him to. We are born creators, but not made for sin.

The duplicity of the world we live in and the multi-layered functionality of our makeup means there is no action we perform based on a thought that does not establish a reality. We really do create by thought and action.

This is also how some demons are created as well, which is why those heavily in spiritual warfare believe casting out demons will fix a believer's sin problem, which is hardly the case as once the believer acts on an ungodly desire, more demons are created to take its place.

Let's break down James' argument:

"When desire conceives…"

There can only be a conception if there is an action. This is true in the natural as well. I believe this is where the believer is the strongest. In the natural, no amount of thought of having a baby will conceive such. But once an action is put behind that thought, we bring a soul into this world. In the same way, we bring the sins we fight against into this world.

Remember what the Bible said, *When Adam sinned, sin came into this world.* In other words, Adam's ungodly act gave birth to something ungodly.

"Be angry, and do not sin": do not let the sun go down on your wrath, nor give place to the devil. Let him who stole steal no longer, but rather let him labor, working with his hands what is good, that he may have something to give him who has need. Let no corrupt word proceed out of your mouth, but what is good for necessary edification, that it may impart grace to the hearers. And do not grieve the Holy Spirit of God, by whom you

were sealed for the day of redemption. (Ephesians 4:26-30 - NKJV).

Therefore submit to God. Resist the devil and he will flee from you. (James 4:7 - NKJV).

Biblical translations do us a bit of injustice sometimes as references to the "devil" is not always about an external entity, but sometimes it points to the internal demons we create and fight with. Every ungodly act creates something ungodly that wants to be fed, and it is not God it desires.

The will is at its strongest when faced with the struggle of desire or temptation. We can tell that girl/boy not to come over. We can change the television channel. We can choose not to take a second look. But if we fail at this level and act, we:

"Give birth to sin…"

At this stage, we have a real problem. We repent sincerely, but the *baby* is still there and has its demands. It wants to be fed, and its diet is strict; a repetition of the very act that brought it into existence. It feels like an intense hunger emanating from the core of your being.

The fight here is intense as the one born from above, which is you, goes to war with the one born from an ungodly act, which is also you. It takes death to be free from the spoilt *baby* crying out for more ungodliness.

I have been crucified with Christ; it is no longer I who live, but Christ lives in me; and the life which I now live in the flesh I live by faith in the Son of God, who loved me and gave Himself for me. (Galatians 2:20 - NKJV).

If we fail at this level, then:

"Sin, when it is fully grown, leads to death..."

Remember, James was writing to believers. Passive Christianity has taken over the Western churches. We want someone else to do the work for us. We forget what God said: "Work out your own salvation with fear and trembling."

The struggle is real for the believer *(I know. I say this a lot)*, but our responsibility remains. Sin crouches at the door, but we must master it.

Conclusion

Too many believers today are struggling with the *unrighteous babies* they gave birth to. It has led to much confusion and to many walking away from God because of their inability to master sin. If there is any area of our walk with God that requires some measure of violence or aggression, this is it.

So if your eye—even your good eye—causes you to lust, gouge it out and throw it away. It is better for you to lose one part of your body than for your whole body to be thrown into hell. And if your hand—even your stronger hand—causes you to sin, cut it off and throw it away. It is better for you to lose one part of your body than for your whole body to be thrown into hell. (Matthew 25:28-30 - NLT).

This is in no way easy to do, and it feels like an injustice to self as we deny that which it wants. We all struggle internally with different personalities and realities of our own making. The first kingdom God gives you to rule is you. You govern the kingdom that is you. You are responsible. Mastering sin is what qualifies you to rule other kingdoms, and even nations.

This is a struggle for us all, but I believe we can do it.

Connect with the author @
malachicsteele@gmail.com

www.ingramcontent.com/pod-product-compliance
Lightning Source LLC
Chambersburg PA
CBHW072056040426
42447CB00012BB/3149